Recluse Freedom

J O H N L E A X

Recluse Freedom

Poems

WORDFARM
SEATTLE, WASHINGTON

WordFarm
2816 E. Spring St.
Seattle, WA 98122
www.wordfarm.net
info@wordfarm.net

Cover Image: iStockphoto
Cover Design: Andrew Craft

USA ISBN-13: 978-1-60226-012-2
USA ISBN-10: 1-60226-012-5
Printed in the United States of America
First Edition: 2012

Library of Congress Cataloging-in-Publication Data

Leax, John.
[Poems. Selections]
Recluse freedom : poems, 1990-2010 / John Leax. -- 1st ed.
p. cm.
ISBN-13: 978-1-60226-012-2 (pbk.)
ISBN-10: 1-60226-012-5 (pbk.)
I. Title.
PS3562.E262A6 2012
811'.54--dc23

2012004156

P 10 9 8 7 6 5 4 3 2 1
Y 17 16 15 14 13 12

Acknowledgments

Poems in this collection have appeared in:

Avocet
Christianity and Literature
The Cresset
Flourish
Ginger Hill Review
Hidden Oak
Image
ISLE
Karamu
Mars Hill Review
The Northern Agrarian
The Other Journal
Stonework
Westview

For Linda: A Little Conversation

I'd like to be a hermit with you.

If I were with you,
you wouldn't be a hermit.

I'd be a happy camper.

Contents

Considered from a Certain Aspect

...each kind of being is in its own way, is good in its own
way, is beautiful in its own way.
—Jacques Maritain (Joseph W. Evans, translator)

The beaver, rippling the still
pond of its own making,
its small paws
feeding the thin branches into its nibbling teeth,
is in its own way—
good and beautiful.

The old, one-eyed man, not striding,
ambling, stopping and starting
on the path,
as his vision beholds and holds him
moved and motionless—What
has he abandoned to be what
he, in his own way, will be?

God knows.

He is *him*self, in his own way,
this moment, good and beautiful,
watched by the rich, red-brown doe
still on the path between
the fringe of cottonwoods
lining the creek like words
and the knee-high corn
that is, in its own way,
like the doe,
good and beautiful.

Writing Home
1990-2002

Home

Even then, before I knew the word
contained more pain than comfort,
I loved the way, when we rode
from Wilkinsburg to East Pittsburgh,
the streetcar, at a certain point,
rattled under the highway
and slipped along the steep tree-
covered hillside beneath the stone bluffs
down into the valley, and the stop
a block above the mile-long Westinghouse
plant, and the transfer to the car
to Turtle Creek.

I loved the way, at that same point,
the highway took to the air,
bridging the streetcar line to scale
the valley side and run along the ridge:
the way, when being driven to grandmother's
and a life I did not understand,
I could look back from my father's car
at the bluffs, where I longed to stand
on the porch of a teetering house
looking out, owning the valley
with my eyes, or stare out the side window
down onto East Pittsburgh and then,
from the wild height of the Westinghouse
Bridge that I sometimes walked, holding
my mother's hand in the wind, see far below
Turtle Creek running its sulfurous way
to the great Monongahela, the Ohio,
and the wondrous Mississippi.

I loved those moments of suspension

in car and streetcar between places,
the sinuous lines of the hills
running away from the crowded valleys,
and the veins of roads connecting
the mysteries of disparate lives
and habitations I knew darkly and in part.

I loved the way, from the streetcar stop,
I knew if I wound up the switch-backing
streets, I would find the Greensburg Pike,
and it would lead to a house where
sleep descended on my eyes and I dreamed
of greater hills and valleys holding
me safely in their folds. And I loved
that the way to that house was a longer walk
than I would make, that that journey
could be accomplished only by another's grace,
and that, though we did not go that way,
once we had, and so I knew we could again.

I loved the way we'd take the number seven
up the street along the plant
(where my grandfather worked) rising
like another bluff over my head
to Turtle Creek itself, and from there
ride the bus along another creek
up Brown Avenue out of town
two or three miles to Leax Lane,
where once I lived in wholeness,
where broken truth occupied a wounded
hill that slowly leaked its orange waters
down and down and down until they ran
under that bridge of suicides and wind,
where I held tight my mother's hand
and made it safe across.

I loved the way, from any point,
I knew the hills and waters were a guide,
that even as they ran off together,
giving up their richness to a delta
far away, I could, by placing one foot
after the other, trust them
to lead me home.

Homecoming

In the beginning there was war,
and my father, hardly more than a boy,
was called. Because he had no church
to witness to the peaceful heart
that spoke a living word within
his chest, he went, and he became
a silent man. In the chasm
of his obedience I fell,
plunged with my first steps
into the wash of blood—a slash
of milky glass split my face from nose
to cheek and left me just one eye to watch
for his return. My mother wept,
I'm sure. No one told my father.
He soldiered on in ignorance of the night
already settling on his day.

His oldest brother fell at Normandy,
and though he rose, he rose to thump
impatiently on one good leg,
on one good stump. My father had no hour
to take such news to heart. Under orders,
he drove forward, sometimes horsing an ammo
truck, sometimes a general's jeep.
He posed for photographs and sent them
like postcards to his wife and mother, joked,
"Having a wonderful time."

Then, one April Sabbath in 1945,
his Easter prayers still moist upon his lips,
he drove into a tomb empty of all purpose:
thirty thousand creeping skeletons,
inhuman, massed like insects behind a fence,

nine thousand heaped bodies, bone rubble,
stacked, meticulously accounted for
in the dark books of Dachau order,
disordered every word he knew. No joke
could force the truth aside. No prayer
he'd learned in the bright bedtimes
of his farm-boy youth could halt the stone
rolling inexorably between the close
enclosure of his mind and the wide
goodness of the life he knew before the word
descended void in vengeance, blood, and bone.

Thirty years from that moment, his heart gave
up the burden of his eyes. He shrugged,
gave a muffled cry, and died. It was night.
My mother's call reached me in morning.

His body lay gravely silent when I stood
to pray beside it. What question I asked,
what answer I sought, I cannot even
now find voice to say. I think, should
God come down to answer for this world,
he too might break his silence with a shrug,
give up, and die, helpless before the blank
enormity he'd meet in flesh.
I wonder if I'd know him in his life
or in his death. The day I met my father
I was three. My aunt held me above the swirl
of eager wives jamming the station hall.
Each time a man, young, joyful, in uniform,
descended from a bus, I cried,
"Is that him? Is that him?"
I can't remember when she said, "Yes,"
or if he took me in his arms
and touched my face with his.

Family Story

The first Christmas I remember, Mother
almost died. A child playing
like a man pointed a shotgun from a window;
the double barrels boomed.

Going up the walk, Mother met
the blast that was not winter
but held more coldness
than the day. She met the blast
and spun backwards
one arm hanging loose,
her face half gone. I remember
how she stumbled through the door
and fell crying on the couch,

"I've been shot."

I remember my father holding her
and the ambulance that came
and went in silence—no siren
to scream the wail I was too dumb-
struck to raise.

And the child playing like a man,
I remember, hid under his bed
and would not come out.

And I remember Christmas Eve,
my father at the laundry tub
scrubbing at the stains in Mother's
clothes. "They won't come out,"
he said, bending, showing me

the marks and tiny pellet holes
I could not number.

And I remember months later
the waiting-room hours I endured
alone, while in the closed office
next door, my father holding
her hands against the pain,
the doctor probed and dug
the dark shot from her body.
He did not get it all.

Some lodged too deep.
Some lodged too close—
this is the truth—
to her heart to be disturbed.

And some—I did not know this—
has waited in my own until this moment
fifty years and more away,
so I sit remembering, wondering
how it was in innocence
I understood so little

I said that night, kneeling
beside the child playing like a man
crawled finally from
his silent darkness:

"Our Father, who art in Heaven...."

The Body of the Lord

Like water, light spilled through the east window,
splashing our faces, soaking our taut bodies
with late summer heat, tempting our hearts, word
weary, to abandon discipline,
to leap free of the young preacher, powerful
in his call, sure in the authority
of his voice, and burst through the open door
to the shadowed grass littered with broken
husks beneath the buckeye tree. But we did
not leap; we plowed, like moles, through the dark
transcendence he spoke, like a new creation,
for us to dwell in. He led us, phrase
by phrase, through the ancient catechism:
"What," he'd question, "is the chief end of man?"
And we, in answer to his urgency,
would cry, "To glorify God and enjoy
Him forever," as if we understood
the bound mystery of the morning.

At noon, when he released us, we fled outside
to sandwiches and punch, to cookies, fruit,
and play. The world came back to us, or we,
lost once more in its glory, reached out
to it. On hands and knees we searched the ground
picking buckeyes from the prickly husks.
We sought perfection, and when we found it,
we pierced it with a pocket knife and strung
it from a knotted thong. We twirled it round
our heads to learn its weight and balance before
testing hand and eye and seed in a game
designed to break the spirit and the flesh.

One player held his buckeye suspended

22

still in humid air. The other whipped
his overhand and tried to smash his friend's
to smithereens. Once I found a nut so hard
to crack it lasted three long days before
it shattered when I struck my blow. It broke
apart, its inedible green meat flying,
sticking to my face and shirt. I tasted
its bitterness and spit it out in haste.
All day, despite the water I swirled and
drank, the faithful taste stuck to my tongue,
as if in tasting I'd taken into
myself the very savor of the earth.

Then, one evening near autumn's fall,
we gathered in our room and stood, like Adam
quaking in his new knowledge, before
the assembled elders of the church.
Outside the open door a spectacle
of fireflies betrayed the solemn wonder
of our examination with silent joy.
We confessed our sinful hearts. The elders
nodded sagely and confirmed us ready.

Sunday afternoon, they broke Christ's body
and for our sin spilled his blood. On silver
trays they passed small squares of bread. In tiny
cups they served us juice. They told us, "Eat.
Drink." The bread was soft. Rolled into
a ball it was easy to swallow, but the juice
was bitter—like the buckeye tang of summer.
When I prayed, my halting tongue confessed
one word, the lasting savor of Creation.

Words

In sun and rain and snow, I walked each day
the long downhill of Forest Avenue.
Beside a narrow swamp-fed creek, I turned
onto a shortcut, red-dog lane to Braddock
Road so steep strong walkers slowed and had
no need to watch for cars. Michael Willing,
my closest sixth grade friend, lived at its end
until his father met a clever girl
at work and found her willing more than he
at first found nerve or wit enough to ask.

A mile past Michael's, Nonny, another friend,
who kept a 'coon he'd trapped himself, lived across
from the park where Doctor Black led our class
and tried to teach us how to name the plants.
Mornings I'd call Michael out. Together
we'd take the weed-rich path tramped clean
through straggly third-growth scrub to Woodside School.

I liked that path. Mornings Michael stood in bed
with flu or fever I liked it best, for then
I walked companioned by imagination.
Those mornings, sunlight, broken by wind-bent trees,
lay shattered, gleaming on the ground. From the shards
shadows reached back to touch the trees. The threat
of dark they threw across my way fell
a pleasing threat should any thought of mine
stray from the packed delineation set
by habit and stern direction to keep my walk
unwavering to school. In that light I knew
a lurking *underpresence* in the wood.
I never turned around to see behind.
The bravest boy I knew, I drove ahead,

my stumbling self receiving courage from
my mindless feet. I thought my way was safe.

That year I fell in love—not with Rita
Hopewell, the bulky girl who sought me out
at every dance and calmed me with her touch
and honey voice. I should have found her fine.
But Heather Steele, the one who cast her smiles
across the room and reeled in boys like small
pond bluegills, claimed my mind and eye.
Her card to me on Valentine's, a great,
lace heart, was signed *with love*. I swallowed hard.
For weeks I thought I owned the one who thrilled
my waking, but after school one day in March,
I found the same card plastered on the wall
in Michael's room.
                    I sneaked a look:
she'd signed it *love*. Michael laughed,
"That's the way love goes," then named
three other fools cherishing the word
she'd emptied with her feckless pen.
A few days later, Michael's mother locked
the door against his father, and quick,
before the spring was fully born,
Michael and his mother fled.

My walk along the daily path became
a different walk. Where once I walked
delighted when solitude accompanied me
by chance, I walked each day alone,
friendship and love forgotten
as leaves closed out the light and spilled
darkness at my feet. No longer was I brave.
Often I ran panting through the shadows,
bounding rabbit-like from left
to right, homing for a thick brush pile

where no dog could dig me out.

Then, one afternoon, walking home,
measuring the rhythm of my steps
in words, I told myself a story;
I made a poem of my fear.
A voice not wholly mine stayed
my urge to run. Word after word, I walked
the wood, and when I stepped onto
the everyday asphalt of Braddock Road,
I stepped into my life, a boy given
to the world both hidden and revealed.

I walked to Nonny's house. I fed a crayfish
to his 'coon, and when I climbed back up
the hill to turn once more down the lane,
I swore I'd dwell in fields like Doctor Black
and name and name and name until, by word,
I found a way to hold the line that lay
a blade between my fear and joy.

Sorrow

Those years I roamed from my father's door
to the limits of an afternoon's ramble
and beyond into the gathering darkness
of evening light, I learned the quiet
ecstasy of chosen loneliness.

I learned in waywardness I will be always
startled by the thunderous flight
of the grouse breaking from the brush,
by the sudden crash of the deer
clearing the briars under the wild apple trees,
by the dry laughter of the blacksnake's
body in the fallen leaves.

I learned in waywardness I have no way to lead
except with my eye, that my hands,
though they long for touch, follow slowly,
and only by the discipline of will do they reach
out to know the hardness of the turtle's shell
warmed by sunlight playing along
the patterned ridges of its mottled back.

I learned in waywardness they will,
undisciplined, recoil from the writhe of sinew,
from muscle, taut with tension, untamed,
alive in the freedom of its splendid separateness.
I learned in sorrow that every living thing,
both small and large, is born to go in fear
and dread of my hungry hands.

I learned that my desire, such love I
can offer, is not enough to calm the frog,
flecked with duckweed, from the shallow pond.

He will not yield his trust to me.
To know even partially his beating life,
I must grasp, hold him in hand or mind
against his will. And so I live, grasping
and yielding, clutching and letting go.

Marriage

Through the dark of storm, in snow
swirling about the rented car
with Florida plates and no winter tires,
we crawled north along the Allegheny
through the National Forest,
over the mountains, onto the glacier-
leveled plateau, and down into the wide
valley of the Genesee, and came unknowing
to what would be our chosen place.

One day married, we drove with everything
we owned piled on the seat behind us.
The gifts of friends held us on the road;
we never spun a tire, but we went
in blindness, our vision stolen
by the wind and our own too easy
acquiescence to our vows. We steered
by wish and the faint line beside us
of utility poles and pasture fences.

We never saw another car. In the glow
of dashboard lights I saw your face
transfigured, but I cannot say
if what I saw was joy at our new union
or storm fear beating at your heart.
I drove elated, a husband fool enough
to trust the headlamps and his hands
to find the way home. I found the way
that night and brought us both to rest.

In morning light we learned the strength
of the storm we'd blundered through.
For days, easy in our love, we stayed

inside, contained by winter's whitest hours.
When the roads, at last, were opened,
we stepped into the cold of everyday
and walked as blindly as we drove
into the darkness of our vows that
neither hands nor lamps could stay.

19 Torpey Street

In the eighth year of our marriage,
we came, parents with our young daughter,
to this house, stark, built in 1900,
stripped of its trim by an early owner
then sided with brittle white shingles.
Liking the thought of never painting,
we paid, by law, the market value
to Ken and Mary Rice, but grace governed
the exchange we made that April day,
voiding the language of deed and contract:
in the west kitchen window Mary left,
hanging by a chain, a hoya, and on
the table maps of her perennial
gardens, planted at the edges
of the quarter-acre grounds. By gift
she made us inheritors of her trust.

Coming with little, we arrived in hope,
confident the richness of our life
together would bear us forward. Behind
we left the dark of paralysis
and silence. We left the brace that let you
step into your day. We left the jumbled
consonants and vowels of the broken
speech you sputtered before you learned
to shape, a second time, a world of words.

We could not, however, leave all behind.
With the few good things we owned—our books,
our bed, our couch, four chairs, and glass-
topped table—we brought knowledge,
not of good or evil, but of the grim fix
of common pain: like Adam and Eve,

expelled from their first security,
we entered the light of our lasting place.

Once, cutting wood with an old man, I asked
about his wealth of energy, "Never
quit," he said, and then went on, "Growing up,
I knew one work—getting ready for winter.
That's life. You get ready. You suffer the cold.
You get ready again." The first summer
we lived on Torpey Street, I lived running
heat lines, hidden from sunlight, crawling
the dirt crawl space of my stone-walled basement.
Deep beneath our lives, breathing the damp earth,
disturbing spiders, and skinning my knuckles
assembling the metal ducts that would carry
warm air to the chilled corners of the wind-
wrapped winter house, I made his words my own.

The house has passed a hundred years,
and we've passed sixty. The dark we carried
fell, passed away, and fell again. We
can't prevent what lies ahead. But here
is our place of suffering, and by Christ
who died, here also is our place of joy.

Mary's hoya blooms wax stars fragrant as oils
to dress the body of the Lord. It thrives in
light. The resurrection comes each spring.

The Garden

We dug our garden first on a neighbor's
land, keeping the back lawn a safe expanse
for Melissa, our daughter, and her friends.
We planted predictable crops: lettuce, beans,
tomatoes, a little corn, broccoli,
and beets. We satisfied our hunger, gave more
than we could eat away, and found a small
economy grown almost apart from
our intent. We liked its work and working.

Our neighbor moved and sold our borrowed plot.
Turned back onto ourselves, we turned our loss
into commitment; spade by spade, we broke
a corner of the playground yard to make
a garden we could keep. Digging, we found
old bottles, shards of earthenware, broken,
rusted tools—screwdrivers, knives, and wrenches—
remnants of lives lived here before our own.

We joined our work to theirs. Planting apple
trees, a row of blueberries, asparagus,
we chose to live in hope of things we could
not see by season's end. We bound ourselves
to steward one small place as in our vows
we bound ourselves to body forth our love.

As Melissa grew the garden grew, spreading
to enclose her place of play within our
place of labor. I waged war with groundhogs,
hurled bullet words at rabbits, and despaired
at slugs rasping the sweet new leaves of beans
with their violent tongues. Some days it seemed
that we would lose it all, but autumn brought

us always to our knees with more than we
could use. Some we froze for winter. Much more
we gave away, and what was left we heaped
into the compost bin to work till spring.

One April, holding in her memory
the wild abundance of fall, my wife spoke,
"Flowers might be nice." The noise I made meant
neither *yes* nor *no*. It meant I did not hear,
but her word woke in me as if I had.
That summer I turned fifty. Melissa
married, and, leaving, left us changed.

Where she had played, I made a crescent bed
between the house and raised plot that holds
our vegetables. In it I dug a pond
for fish and lilies. I lined its edge with
stone hauled from the woodlot creek and planted
shrubs, flowers, herbs: barberry, spirea,
hydrangea, coreopsis, mint, thyme, phlox,
and, inviting wildness in, red bee balm
for hummingbirds and butterflies.

At the limit of our deed, I planted
a hedge enclosing our domestic
habitation. In time finches claimed it
for their own, making our limit open
to more than we can know. Within that hedge
I built a place for words, a cabin, small
and tight, like a poem crafted from years
of silence. I go there mornings and keep
my peace. In summer, birds fill the window,
skitter on the roof. In winter, when wind
stirs the lilac branches, the scraping
on the hemlock wall becomes music, one song
Creation sings in cold. Another song

I make, scratching these words across my page.
By grace and good intention the songs are
one, a contrapuntal fugue of measured
lines, the garden beds, and patterns wildly
scored by bird flight on the sky. Enclosed
by vow and years of labor, broken soil mounds
in fertile beds, its depth our blessed end.

The Woods

The woods is not itself, independent, free
of history. It is a wildness in the heart
of culture, a wildness shaped by human
hand, by insect, water, wind, and time.
A ragged square bound by road, pasture, field
and sprawl of houses creeping up the hill
from town, it lives because we chose to give
a name to it before we knew its nature.
We called it *Remnant Acres* and brought
to life a place apart from habitation
where hemlock, ash, and maple could stand
free of market value.

                    An old fence line
marks the northern boundary, keeping horses
from the apples fallen where once an orchard
thrived. It is now a scattering of twisted
trees favored by deer who browse low sweeping
branches when winter settles on the hill.
I've cut a few to ease my winter woes
as well and warmed our room with apple flames
and cider. I've even fed on apple-fat
venison compliments of hunting friends.
These small assertions by deer and human
make to the woods no never-mind. It takes
them as they come, unbidden and unnoticed.

Beyond the orchard, a seep-damp slope
tempts me always to build a pond, to turn
raspberry-popple thicket into sun-
reflected water and make a landscape
fitted to my eye. Our active naming
prevents me, holds me to my word, my choice
to see here my willfulness disciplined

by what is real before me, to find my heart's
desire outside myself. Here, even
in summer, I walk with wet feet, pushing
through brambles, stepping over logs turning
slowly—within their solid shapes—to soil.
All that is is becoming something else,
just as I am changing within my body,
by word and deed, into a part of all
I cannot know except by walking here.

The seep gathers into a flow and runs down
into a little brook. So grounded, water
begins its journey back to rain. I walk
the summer-dry bank plunged deep in memory
of skunk cabbage pungent with spring.
Hemlocks loosed by undercutting floods lie
in my way. Blocked, I step around or duck
beneath them. How quietly the Maker
of this place chooses to be beside me,
invites me from the bank into the stream
of shaping water. In them my walk becomes
a leaping dance from stone to tumbling stone,
a formal yielding within the wildness
we have chosen to keep ourselves alive.
Each time I give myself to find its grace,
it leads me back to where my walk begins—
to you and to our common hold on earth.

Bright Wings
1995-2005

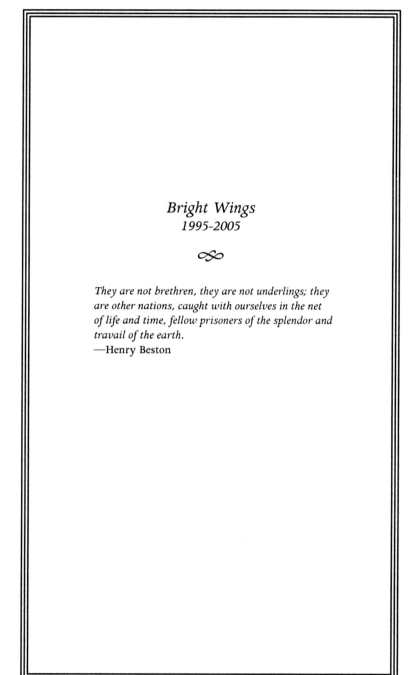

They are not brethren, they are not underlings; they
are other nations, caught with ourselves in the net
of life and time, fellow prisoners of the splendor and
travail of the earth.
—Henry Beston

Dance

At the drip line of the apple tree, a bird
kicked up snow as if it were
bathing in dust. In the unsteady light,
I called the bird a dove.

Its head bobbed sharply up and down.
Rising puffs of white rose over it
as it slowly turned, leaving the yard
imprinted as if by angel wings.

A dark third wing, previously
hidden, emerged from the drift,
as if a second bird were dancing
close against its breast.

The wing twitched once, twice,
as if it would catch the air
or repel the closeness of its striking
partner. And then the dance came round.

A sharp-shinned hawk looked up.
He shifted, stabbed the snow,
lifted a winter-olive goldfinch
in his beak and flew.

I stood in the window. The emptied
imprints filled with light.

Landscape with Crows

This is no Japanese landscape
with herons poised along a water's edge.
This is New York.

Still, the beaver pond spreads
like an ink wash.
Stumps break its surface,
and one tree, stripped of bark
but soundly branched, rises
fifty yards from shore.

In opposite forks, two pairs
of herons nest. One pair is lining
its ragged dish of sticks
with needles ripped from a white pine
on the shore where I sit watching.
The other is using grass.

They have made a ritual of their work.
First one flies. Its strong, slow-motion
wingbeats write a fine iambic
on the sky. Landing,
it marks a clear caesura
and fills its beak with softness

before rounding out the line and ending
back where it began. There,
it stands and offers to its mate
what it has gathered.
And then they trade. The mate repeats
the line that sings the morning's promise.

Across the pond, poised in silhouette

in the hemlocks massed along the shore,
three crows confer and wait.

Spring Herons

A dozen Canada geese patrol
the wind-rough pond.
Snow, untouched by sun, sinks
slowly into the woods floor.
Change is clear and near,
but the mosquito whine
of a farmer's chainsaw
drills the mind with truth.
What has been will be once more.

Above it all, in the single
tree rising barkless from
the pond's dark safety,
two herons stand in nests
of tangled sticks. Their
slender necks folded tight
to their breasts, they
are as gray and still as
the deadwood at their feet.

The upper bird moves. Her long
beak is too bright, tropically
garish, almost orange against
the brooding sky. She strokes one
side of it and then the other
against the smooth trunk.
Lifting her wings, shrugging
aside the persistent cold,
she swells to twice her size.

The other bird, her black
eye-stripe as still as a shadow,
betrays no eagerness. The light

will lengthen out the day and
what will come to her will come.
I watch, fixed on staying
still at least until she moves,
but she outstrips my kind
desire. I cannot hold my peace.

Then suddenly the upper bird
reaches her beak high, stretching
her neck like a pointer at a word
written on a screen. Poised so,
she steps into the air. My eyes
follow her. Her wings work slowly.
Her neck folds back on her breast,
and I am held, as she is in her
flight, by unimaginable grace.

A Bird in the Hand

That spring day the evening grosbeak
stunned itself crashing into the window
and fell twitching, its feet
like small forked sticks sticking
up at the all-accepting sky,
we should have taken a photograph.

That spring day I lifted from the bed
of seed beneath the window near the feeder
the evening grosbeak, and held in my hands
the stunning gold of its weightless body,
and touched the fierce mask blackening
its eye, we should have taken a photograph.

That spring day I sat on the deck's edge
beneath the apple tree beside the feeder,
and waited for the evening grosbeak
to slowly right itself and stand
quietly, almost as if trusting, on my open
hand, we should have taken a photograph.

That spring day when, after one half hour,
the evening grosbeak walked carefully
from my palm and sat at my side
on the deck and, almost as if trusting,
allowed me to stroke its shining back,
we should have taken a photograph.

That spring day, in the moments before
the telephone called me from such
intimacy as could be taken only as a grace,
before the evening grosbeak come to its
senses took wing and lifted itself away,

we should have taken a photograph.

That spring day, in the eternity
of the evening grosbeak's presence,
in the flashing of God's acceptance of his
fallen creature when lifted by grace,
any photograph we should have taken
would only have held a bird in hand.

Two Rose-Breasted Grosbeaks

He is wearing formal black
but sporting,
above the starched white
of his chest,
a blood ascot.

She is, as always, demure—
quietly herself, marked
with bold eyebrows
and russet streaks
all down her breast.

He is putting on a show:
his right wing is half spread,
dragging through the seeds
fallen to the deck
from the feeder.

He is vulnerable, injured,
broken.
Pathetically, he approaches her,
turns away, returns,
bows imploring.

Then, nonchalantly,
devil-may-care,
he flies to a blossom-
bright limb
of the apple tree.

All this for love?

All this for love.

Orioles

An oriole sings from the hedge.
—Jane Kenyon

Here, in the hedge-enclosed garden
I inhabit, orioles come
and go. Other birds, more ordinary
yet stunning in their feathered hues,
sing from bush and tree.

A wren, warbling his *love me*
song from beanpole height,
wearies us if not his mate. A cardinal
trills his aria of ownership
from sugar maple crown,
while murmuring doves step
down the roof and finches,
common as sparrows,
chitter at sunflower seeds.

But our orioles, coming and going,
do not sing. As I watch, one
swoops into the yard, sets
the plastic orb of nectar
swinging, and briefly satisfies
its need. It ratchets a burning
whir from its throat, then flames
through sunlight to the drooping
cover of a creek-side willow
beyond the boundary hedge.

Nearby, a contralto robin
gathers peony blossoms
to line her larch-hidden nest.

In all this song, my searching eye,
like the swinging feeder,
pendulums to stillness.

Surprise

See. There. Quick.
The hummingbird
motionless
on the dead spruce branch
above the bee
balm flame.

She is no blur
of wings.

And look.
Her long nectar-
loving beak—
She has tucked it
in the feathers
of her breast.

A Crow in Light

One morning in the summer rising
light of the garden, I sat reading
of Isaiah and the wilderness.
He foretold, as well as lions
bedding with lambs, jackals
in the palace, hyenas in the square.

As I read, a rose-breasted grosbeak
at the feeder broke sunflower seeds,
dropped the husks, and blackened
the lilies sending up their stalks.

Above my head in the larch,
the jays began. Their jeering fell
like stabs of icy hail. High in the tree
a soft branch shivered, bare twigs
snapped under an assault of wings.
Screeching filled the air,
and a crow broke into light.

The jays followed, screaming, plunging
at the awful back. The crow,
inscrutable, lumbered off, its beak
dangling a sack of chick.

The sky emptied, fell silent.
I returned to my book.
The grosbeak cracked another seed.

Faith in a Seed

And now, late summer, the young
robins marching about
displaying speckled breasts
and fierce dispositions,
the starlings spaced evenly
along the power lines anticipating
the rush of artic winds,
the goldfinch males, brilliant
in their patience, mounting the purple
sumac and calling their olive mates
to love, for now is seedtime.
The flowers, spent, spend all
their wealth to buy another season
from the cold, and the finches,
nesting late and well, find
in the wild dispersion
the satisfaction of every want
they neither know nor question.

Bright Wings

Above the branches overhanging
trail and river gorge, vultures wove
the sky. As they arced,
the dark muscles of their flesh
held steady. Their feathers
contained and spilled the sunlight
striking at their underwings.

Round they went, the circles
of their soaring moving east and west,
north and south, as if some order
moved them in the light.

Once, and once again, a single bird
spun from the gyre, streaked through
the spruce tops, then, brilliant
in the wind, lifted far above the land
to join again the silent tumult
of their *ah! bright wings*.

Great Horned Owl

Sometimes, late, reading
in the soft hope
of a single bedside lamp,
I hear the great horned owl
haunting Mouth of the Creek.

I have seen him there dazed
in sunlight, sullen, among crows
in a leaning cottonwood.

Sometimes, lifting my eyes
to the night, I would lift also my voice
and call sharply as he does,
hoo hoo-oo hoo hoo,
but once, half-awake by a campfire,
I was screamed upright by a rabbit
meeting that fall in the dark,
and I could not name
that goodness as my own.

Tonight, downed in comfort,
I raise this call apart—
these words separate and clear:
Whatever is is good.

Recluse: An Adirondack Idyll
2004

*The lands of the state, now owned or hereafter
acquired, constituting the forest preserve, as now
fixed by law, shall be forever kept as wild forest
lands. They shall not be leased, sold, or exchanged,
nor shall any timber be sold, removed or destroyed.*
—Article XIV, Section 1, New York State
Constitution

*It's no damned PARK.
It's the ADIRONDACKS.
It's our HOME.
We work here.*
—Adirondack bumper sticker

Recluse

> For Chinese intellectuals, living as a recluse did not normally
> mean living the ascetic life of an isolated hermit. Instead it
> meant a highly cultivated life in a secluded mountain setting,
> complete with family and visiting friends.
> —David Hinton, The Mountain Poems of Hsieh Ling-yun

When the Vanderbilts purchased Sagamore from William West
Durant, they constructed an outdoor bowling alley on a rein-
forced concrete slab that withstood an earthquake. The archi-
tectural originality of the camp, however, was all in the façade.
Nothing of substance was effected. Nor was the life original.

One of the tasks of their servants, who lived out of sight, was to
greet guests by setting off fireworks as they arrived.

At Star Lake in the shadow of Maple Mountain, I live with my
wife in a four-room cabin. Were it at Sagamore, it would be in
the servants' village. On the wall beside our door a sign identi-
fies the cabin as *Sparrows' Nest*. This comforts me, for the Psalm-
ist writes, "Even the sparrow finds a home," and Jesus himself
proclaims, "Are not two sparrows sold for a penny? Yet not one
of them will fall to the ground apart from your Father." I live
here apart, a temporary resident, and work contentedly, secluded
in this mountain setting. Friends visit my wife.

What name should we give this place we call for so short a time
our home? Shall we call it a wilderness containing a garden walled
against the wild? Or is it the One vast garden holding the wild we
must preserve to know our lives originally?

Is it of any consequence that Durant died a pauper, that Vanderbilt
was lost at sea? Is it safe to ascend a height?

Star Lake Night

Open the door and step onto the porch.
The night may well be spread before you.
The stars may lie in the water.
The fox cry may waken you to dreams.

The night may well be spread before you,
or mounded clouds obscure the dark.
The fox cry may waken you to dreams,
or frighten you to sleep once more.

The mounded clouds may obscure the dark.
Clouded, you may stand abandoned.
Frightened, you may sleep once more.
Your only surety is risk.

Clouded, you may stand abandoned.
The stars may lie in the water.
Your only surety is risk.
Open the door and step onto the porch.

Eclipse

The moon did not climb through the trees; the trees rather stood in front of it, laying dark lines against its face and shadows on the light-washed ground at my feet. The same shadows probably lay up and down my body, but I never looked at myself. The night was sensuous, the October cold more a quality of the light than of temperature. I stood comfortably in shirtsleeves.

Earth's shadow caught the moon and pulled its fullness out of shape before it reached the open sky. It held it close, covered it, and as the darkness deepened, reduced its presence to a soft orange glow.

The only sound was wind as subtle as a habit's fabric brush during prayer. Such vespers! The stars multiplied, millions of years' shining against the white spill of the Milky Way.

Then black, black, like lightless stars, leading rolls of crescendoing thunder, three fighter jets swarmed in the night.

Praying the Psalms in Adirondack Park

When I was first in these mountains, I stayed only a short time. I climbed Algonquin in the bright turning of October. Snow closed me in, shutting out every view, and I needed a compass to find my way across the glacier-stripped summit to the trail I descended into a state torn by the Vietnam War.

I have come to the mountains, this time, to keep a longer watch, to see summer pass into fall and fall into winter. In sunlight, I have climbed three mountains. In mist and thunderstorm, I have paddled two rivers. Through the thunderstorm, I sat like a troll in a culvert passing under a road reaching to the edge of wilderness. Wet and dry, I rejoiced.

After each outing, however, I have returned to my small cabin to find waiting news of a present war. I read accounts of deaths mounting up, the ones we count and the ones we do not count because they are not ours. I read the words of the president who tells me we are winning. Democracy will come to Iraq, he assures me, as long as we stay the course and support the troops.

Two miles from where I write these words, pale green paint flakes from vacant buildings, and the open pit of the Jones and Laughlin iron mine lies filled with water. Loons nest at the edges of its undisturbed peace. A few miles farther up the road, at Newton Falls, a solitary watchman and his dog patrol the empty paper mill, protecting the interests of a distant corporation.

Some mornings, I wake to low rumblings and look out on a sun-splashed lake. The shaking earth tells the artillery at Fort Drum is practicing. Other mornings all is still. I look out on the mist rising from the water, the sound of the night-flying geese strong in my ears. I raise my eyes to the hills. *From whence cometh my help?*

Meeting the Bear

Adirondack bears, I'm told, do not attack humans. They run away. They have, however, no sure sense of purposeful flight and sometimes run directly at, sometimes run over, what they are fleeing. This knowledge, I suspect, would prove small comfort should a bear choose flight down a trail I'm coming up.

One late summer day descending from the summit of a small mountain, I discovered a pile of bear scat centered in the jeep trail I walked. It hadn't been there an hour before when I'd gone up. I considered it carefully. It was lichen green, firm, and filled with berry seeds. Without bending I could smell it. Surprisingly, in the open air, though it was wild and rank, it was not offensive.

It occurred to me on that mountainside that I was inhabiting, in a literary sort of way, a genre poem, say one by Gary Snyder.

> Kind Bear: Don't mind me;
> you can have the trail
> and the berries too, if you want.

A paw print in the soft earth beside the tire-hardened track suggested the bear had crossed my path and gone on. I had no reason to fear it was ahead of me. I had no reason to fear if it were, but as I stood there, whatever I was feeling felt a lot like fear. Today, reflecting, I wonder. Might what I felt have been anticipation, a trembling readiness to be bowled over, tumbled, and roughed up, by an unspeakable, furry joy?

Life List

I have a friend who is red/green colorblind. He is also an expert
birder and has been accused of waking a whole campground,
calling owls in the dark of early morning. I myself am half-blind,
have no depth perception, and can't tell a hairy from a downy
woodpecker unless they're perched side by side on a yardstick.
Nevertheless I'm an enthusiast and doggedly pursue the little
brown jobbers he so easily names.

"Those aspens are full of yellow-rumps," he'll say. I'll strain
to catch a motion. Sometimes I'll see a shadow and reply, "Oh,
yeah, I see it." And I do see it—more or less—but not well
enough to write it on my list. I'm strict about what I write.

One afternoon we canoed the Oswegatchie to the Chaumont
Swamp. I saw the herons and the loons, and I could name the
waxwings, but the flycatchers and that other bird, the name of
which I've forgotten, on the standing snag an eighth of a mile
away, I only saw disappearing into the woods. The same with
the red-shouldered hawk planing almost invisibly just below the
meeting of the tree line and the sky. I never saw it.

I mostly believe my friend and trust his naming, but now and
then I suspect, particularly when he's naming warblers, that
half of what he sees flies in an imagination he shares with Roger
Tory Peterson and David Allen Sibley. Then I feel bad. Not about
doubting him; a little skepticism becomes a friendship. It's the
doubt I feel about myself—the possibility it's not my eye that
lets me down but something incurable, a disease, a misalignment
of my in-sight with the imagination that makes the world.

for Alan Belford

Climbing Arab in My Sleep

The fire tower that had shuttered in the wind and made me fear its height the first time I climbed Mt. Arab had been replaced with a squat wood structure rising just above the trees to provide a view. Disappointed and curious, I entered it, ascended a single flight of stairs, climbed through a trapdoor in the floor, and stepped into a large room. Windows allowed me to look east to Ampersand and south toward Blue Mountain, but I felt no elation, nothing of the wild exposure of the tower I anticipated. Picnic tables lined the walls and I found myself standing in a concession.

"How much is a sweet roll?" I asked.
"Twenty-one dollars," the attendant told me.
"No thanks, I'll pass," I said.
"They're very large," he answered.

I don't remember buying anything, but I sat at one of the tables talking with a faceless friend. We weren't aware of any motion, but the view out the window changed, and we realized the room was slowly turning. Soundlessly it lifted off the first storey, swept far out from the mountain, and soared like a raven on the wind over Lake Arab.

How that square box could fly I had no idea, but I felt safe. Only the strangeness of the flight and a touch of motion sickness troubled me. Then the room went into a steep dive (though nothing on the tables spilled) and skimmed along the mountain's side. When the flight ended, I stepped from the room onto an asphalt walk through a grove of spruce. Tourists in casual clothes chattered and stepped up to a window to buy snacks. I joined them.

Matins

You rise, awakened by light, at dawn.
You would speak some word to praise creation.
A steel-gray mist hides the lake.
You stand in the no man's land of language.

You would speak some word to praise creation.
The directness of your love demands silence.
You dwell in the no man's land of language.
What truth you know is slant.

The directness of your love demands silence.
The morning is splendid in frost.
What truth you know is slant.
The joy of the morning breaks over you.

The morning is splendid in frost.
The steel-gray mist hides the lake.
The joy of the morning breaks over you.
You rise, awakened by light, at dawn.

Mountain Literature

On the sunlit rock of Ampersand, I rest in history. In 1858, representing The Adirondack Club, William James Stillman paid $600 for the 22,000 acres spread below me. That year the summit was still fully treed. Had he not fallen on Wachusett, Emerson would have answered with his body, as I have, the invitation ringing with a mountain echo. Had not war broken the intention to build a lodge, the poet and his philosopher friends would have continued the talk embracing a sympathy so large as the one they found at Follensby, and all that I survey would be the old growth of their conversation.

The year before he bared this granite heap in 1864, Verplank Colvin wrote "Few understand what the Adirondack wilderness really is. It is a mystery even to those who have crossed and recrossed it by boats along its avenues, the lakes; and on foot through its vast and silent recesses."

What should be said of Colvin, I do not know, but this is true: He loved these mountains awkwardly. Triangulating, measuring and mapping in his rapture of discovery, he scalped mountain after mountain, giving the peaks to wind and rain. Loggers followed quickly.

When fires spread through careless slash, rangers set a watchman in a tower, but they built his cabin fifteen hundred vertical feet below the summit. For eight years in the teens and twenties, Walter Channing Rice, the Hermit of Ampersand, maintained wooden steps, railings, and stone stairs he'd constructed to the summit to speed his daily climb. One summer, sixteen-year-old Bob Marshall, making the ascent, bagged his first Adirondack peak.

In *50 Hikes in the Adirondacks* Barbara McMartin laments the current trail. She calls it "rooted and rutted, with slippery mud in a few precipitous sections," and warns against any illusions that one might be in a pristine wilderness. Other writers declare there is no wilderness and deconstruct constructions.

Bear Mountain

The morning is overcast, hiding the distant mountains, promising rain, but a friend from home has come to climb with me. My heart leaps up: he too carries a stick to spare his knees and help him over rocks.

The trail ascends from the shore of Cranberry Lake. It opens to no views and is only occasionally steep. Three bearded, young hikers with full packs pass us going down. When we reach the lean-to halfway up, the ashes in the fire pit are still warm. Fresh graffiti has been drawn on a rock. It is not witty. My friend, who grew up in these mountains, fills the day with stories of other peaks, of encounters with ruddy, half-dressed hikers, out for conquest. Our accepting laughter trails behind our steps.

At the summit we find a small dome of rock surrounded by trees. We climb onto it and sit. "I like this mountain," my friend announces. We break out our water bottles, slice apples and cheese. *Who are we? What are we doing, two comic, old men perched on a mountain on a day that looks like rain?*

Descending, we do not retrace our steps. We go over the mountain and circle down its far side. At the ledges we stop to view the lake. To our left—Brandy Brook Flow. To our right—Dead Creek Flow. Between them, far out in the water, Joe Indian Island almost disappears in the gray-blue light. And beyond, Cat Mountain rises a tinted shadow that may or may not be real. I like this lake, dissolving in the mist, better than I liked the lake I crossed yesterday, blinded in sunlight, gazing up from the boat looking for these ledges invisible in the trees.

for Bob Blake

Star Lake Morning

Look! Across the lake the mist is rising.
Say what the morning brings to you.
The lone canoeist is not cut loose.
Voices tether him to shore.

Say what the morning brings to you.
A woman waves to the paddler.
Her voice tethers him to shore.
The two become a clarity in sunlight.

A woman waves at the paddler.
Though you can discern no words,
the two remain a clarity in sunlight.
Rejoice in the dazzle of the day.

Though you can discern no words,
the canoeist has not cut loose.
Rejoice in the dazzle of the day.
Look across the lake. The mist has risen.

Benson Mines

Along the Little River, early nineteenth-century road build-
ers found their compasses showing a significant deviation from
north. Speculating the cause was an iron deposit, two friends
purchased 3,400 acres of forest. For 15 years they sold the trees
for railroad ties. Then, having accumulated sufficient capital,
they began to mine. At the height of operations after World War
II, the Jones and Laughlin Corporation, paying royalties to the
friends' descendants, hauled 80 carloads of ore a day to the mill
in Pittsburgh where my uncles worked.

Riding by the mills in my childhood, I thrilled to the fiery blasts
of the night furnaces, when we would return home from family
visits to the airport where we had paid a quarter to stand on the
observation deck and watch lumbering passenger planes take off
and land. As evening fell I would turn away from the runways
to the slagheaps and the railroad cars atop them, silhouetted
against the sky. Fire spilled like lava down the ashy mountain
slope when they dumped their glowing loads.

This morning I rattled through a dying town in a dying van
and drove to the top of the iron mountain left when Jones and
Laughlin closed. No flames threatened me, but as I looked the
two miles down the water-filled pit, across the highway dividing
the tailings pile from the silicon mound sprouting lichens, moss,
grasses and young gray birch, and on to the designated wilder-
ness beyond, I felt the hard hours of laboring families rising
from the abandoned ore.

What can I, a lover of the wild, say to them? The pit below me,
lined with autumn gold and a rock face shining in the sun, lay
like the American sublime painted by Church.

Think of it—the fierce beauty of human industry: from this hole in the ground: 500 local workers and their families. My uncles, aunts, and cousins. The city of smoke and steel. The wealth and security of the nation. The poetry of Williams, Pound, Rexroth, Merton, and Snyder. Words of iron, rocks on which we build.

The Upshot

*In 1899 trapper and guide Reuben Cary killed a wolf in St.
Lawrence County. This was the last documented native wolf
ever taken in New York. After it was stuffed and mounted,
Cary posed with it for a commemorative photograph.*
—Phillip G. Terrie, Wildlife and Wilderness, p. 117

Some want the wolf restored to the Adirondacks.

Some believe it has restored itself. Within the three months
I've been here, two people I trust to trust their eyes have told
me they've seen a wolf. My field guide, however, is skeptical:
"Each year there are a number of reported sightings in the Ad-
irondacks. Even dead wolves have been found, though experts
believe they were released pets."

Carl Sandberg, that wolfish man with sheepdog hair who
claimed a wilderness within himself, once described an expert as
a fool away from home. Far from home myself, I've no opinion.

One morning I was awakened by a sharp bark followed by what
seemed to be panic-driven yelping and a caterwauling I couldn't
believe. For a moment I thought every puppy in the county was
being thrashed with a stick. Adirondack coyotes, I've learned,
are big, considerably larger than their western cousins, and
make a lot of noise. My skeptical field guide reports, "Initial
findings [of scientific studies] indicate that the coyote, on its
journey eastward through southern Canada during the early part
of this century, interbred with timber wolves."

There's more than one way to sneak into the country.

Proximate Thoughts

As the planet turns its back on the sun,
Star Lake hauls down the flowered sky.
A wake like petals trails the evening boat
thrumming slowly into a farther dark.

Thrumming slowly into that farther dark,
your heart would answer the laughing loon,
Or perhaps, turning its back on light, spin
wildly on a doubtful axis and break.

Spinning, doubtful on your broken axis,
you would fix your eye on the solid shore,
hold fast the watery horizon doubled
in the mirrored sky of the flowered lake.

In the flowered sky of the shining lake,
the laughing loon eludes your seeking eye.
No stillness calms your doubt-full heart.
The planet turns its back on the sun.

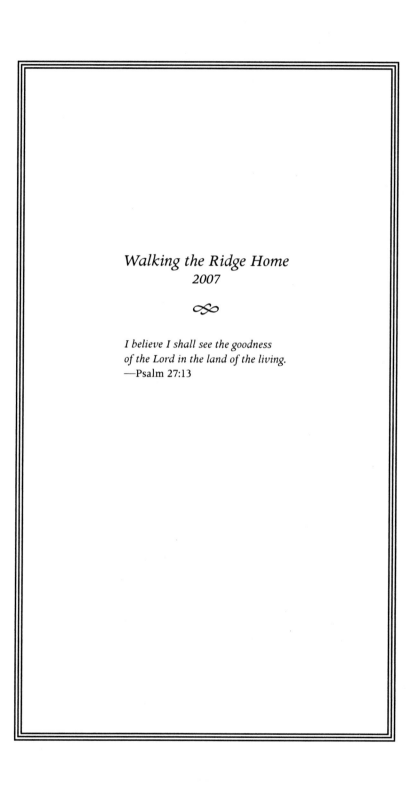

Walking the Ridge Home
2007

∞

*I believe I shall see the goodness
of the Lord in the land of the living.*
—Psalm 27:13

One

With my whole heart I want to praise Thee

In snow   calf-deep   I climb the ridge through pioneer forest—
the trees

thorn apples crowding the field's edge
yield ground under shadowing black cherry ash
and straight white oak

the river at my back
frozen in February light   a promise imagination claims in darkness

    Here I have kicked grouse exploding
    from sheltering drifts
    and jumped back delighted in surprise

    And I have tracked turkey following the arrows
    of their feet backwards
    to the high ground of their roosts

On this cold day
in the wind descending to the tallest oaks

the tallest oaks yielding
as if called
            (obedient to the leading)
arc rooted trails against the silver sky

I place my feet with care
plunge my stick through the sharp crust
to find the holding earth
heart pounding   breathe   breathe

through the trees   arcing
in the wind   turning on the ridge

in the surrounding light

the light of the valley
the light above me
the light below me

Two

Oh darken not to me Thy light

The descent beckons—
      the heart prints trail away
           from the narrow path

half filled
      obscured in the time of their passing
           by the dust of snow
I follow

Under the hemlocks
      the down sweeping branches
           catching my watch cap

lifting it lightly

snow   imperturbably cold
like a leather collar
on the back of my neck
when I release the branch
from my hand

The inclusive silence of the wood
contains the day's vernacular
as the sky contains the silver light

      the hollow thunk
      of woodpecker pounding

      the combustive thrum of cars
      in the valley

foot steps

even the wind
     if it blows
          through the oak tops

like the acorns
     falling into shade
          has no given word

to liven the dumb darkness
of the grove

Three

Teach us dear Lord to number our days

1.
Where the ground falls away
paying the debt
of the steep slope
logged and forgotten

the charred remains of fire
                a circle of stone

a tent of deadfalls
tossed against an oak
              adequate perhaps
                  to shelter
a saint at prayer

2.
Where the apples grow
       gnarled
            and tart

so good every autumn
walk
       strays to bite
again
       that clean flesh
of the lost garden

3.
Where the plantation pines

rise in afternoon light—

a convocation of crows
insolent in shining
regalia mobs
        the mouse-satisfied
           owl

Four

O satisfy us early with Thy mercy

At the edge of this opening in the woods
the poplars
           I declare with the Psalmist

lift up their arms in elegant leaflessness
praising you with the white sheen of their bark
with their rooted journeys in the wind
with the crooked fingers of their hands
spread to receive the blessing of your snow

O that I might stand in their silent choir
a stilled voice going like them no where in the whirl
of the world turning in time

O that I might be mindless of the loss
that has brought me to this place of your making
and unmaking

But you have made me mindful
filled my mouth with words to name
the crow the owl the mouse
you have made me mindful
to love the predator and prey
to taste on my tongue the sacrament
all creation eats
           one life for many

Five

Establish Thou the work of our hands

Oikos—earthhold
the kingdom of God
the economy of culture

      minding the world
      a burl of words

white pine in rows
even aged

(stepping down to the little stream
                        descending
from the far slash
of quick profit)

work of the passing mind
intending renewal

Commercially difficult

poorly formed
      unacceptable
         growing stock

      Harvest is recommended   Removal of inferior pine
      of highest importance   Openings can be made
      where hardwood introduction has begun

In the cathedral light of failure become
shade I stand stilled in ambition's end

On the snow
        banked beside me
a pile of bones
        disarticulated
and in the stream
the bridge
drawn down

by water's mindless
inclination
to fall

Six

Let all the tumult within me cease

I know O Lord you speak in words made flesh
              in the *chick-a-dee dee*
sounding from the thicket
              in the canopy creak of the oaks
straining for the light
              in water slushing
under ice

With my whole heart
              I would serve you
serve you with my finest praise
lifting as freely as mist from the snow

but words lodge homeless
in my throat

Once long ago in the Siskiyous I crossed
open scree near a mountain's summit

Far to the south
        Shasta rose
              luminous
the hope
        of Paradise
              in California cloud

I sucked—in one breath—

the emptiness
the terrible beauty of your way

O how can I know you
how comprehend what mystery caused
you to speak once in word
and once in flesh

O So Close Disclosing
Knowing If Not Known

I am all longing

Speak

Seven

This dwelling, O God, by Thee be blest

If you should take back your Spirit Lord
and gather to yourself your breath
all   all would perish

      the little stream plunging
      like laughter
      into the larger creek cutting this opening
      in the ridge rising
      from the ancient bed
      of the distant river

      the hemlock grove
      shielding its flow
      heavily stocked
      in need of future treatment

      the hardwood stand
      rising in light on the gentler slope
      around the point
      white oak hickory ash
      well spaced for optimum growth

      the orioles who hang their nests
      and sing bright splashes
      in the leafing tops each spring

      these words I say
      giving up all claim
      to make with them
      any world not made

already by your grace

my friend walking here in autumn swelter
"One could make this a place of worship"

Up the knobby spine
                    Thy kingdom come
I place my feet with care
                    Thy will be done
plunge my stick through the sharp crust
                    on earth
heart pounding   breathe   breathe

through the trees   arcing
in the wood bending word
                    as it is
climbing home

in the surrounding light

the light of the valley
the light above me
the light below me
the light of the world
                    forever and ever

Joy   Joy

for Shirley Mullen

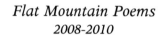

Flat Mountain Poems
2008-2010

*The geography of Flat Mountain has never been
described. It can be located on no map. Existing
nowhere and everywhere, it rises, as Thoreau said,
where ever one is enabled to apprehend within the
perpetual instilling of illusion the real.*

*I've found it, now and then, rising from the bank of
the Genesee River, at a place once known as Mouth
of the Creek.*

Flat Mountain Lost and Found

Hidden heights rise
over landscapes unimagined
by loquacious travelers.

Bears rake blueberries
with gentle claws
and growl approvingly
when one approaches empty
of voracious thought.

Go away or come.
It does not matter.

Who isn't already
at Flat Mountain
is surely lost.

On Flat Mountain Summit
with Josie and Ernie

Children wander Flat Mountain without thinking.
Josie and Ernie hang out with Uncle Jack:
pick green beans in the garden,
tell endless tales,
ask too many questions,
snitch blueberries.

Uncle Jack says, "Umm,"
keeps pulling weeds.
"Watch out for bears,"
he says. "Silly," they say,
"There aren't any bears."

"No bears? Must be this trickster
mountain fooling me with rocks
and light." Laughter rolls across
the great wide rock.

People dwelling in
Mouth of the Creek hear thunder,
hunch their shoulders,
stay inside.

While Massaging My Arthritic Hands, I Consider the Advice of St. Augustine

Trimming the limber forsythia
overhanging the path to the garden
study leads to swollen knuckles
and painful hands.

Splitting firewood does the same.

Staying in the study grasping
the pen turning words about
is just as bad. It's worse.
It swells my head like
a pumpkin watered to bursting.

What shall I do?

Pick blueberries?
Walk at night?
Circumambulate the mountain?

Whatever.

A Scrap of Paper

1.

A friend brought us firewood in the autumn, not enough to fully heat the house, but enough for the small stove we now burn evenings and on weekends after I've walked alone the snowy ridge above the river.

> This cold morning—
> icicles in my beard
> wrinkles in my skin

Clarified, I twist old poems into tight sticks to start the flames.

> My coals?
> Ha!
> Ignite your own heart.

2.

The same friend gave me rough-sawn hemlock from his mill to replace the raised beds in my vegetable garden. In early spring, before the ground was warm, I laid out a new design on a scrap of paper. It took a month to realize it on the ground. From leftover boards I made an arbor for an entrance and a gate decorated with an oversized painted tulip.

> My garden folly—
> speculation
> in petals!

3.

Enriched by compost, the beds were quickly overgrown, the hemlock hidden beneath thick foliage.

Defended by tiny needles
the squash vines
climb where they will

In the groundhog trap
the slug-gnawed broccoli
becomes irresistible

Beetle after beetle
jagged feet clinging
to my fingers
I cleanse the garden

4.

It was my desire to retire without followers, to live companioned
by my books and poems among these vegetables, flowers, and
fruit.

It was not meant to be—
children nibble the sorrel
claiming my path

It was my desire to be awake to the smallest movement of insect
or bird, to make maintenance holy, to find every task a medita-
tion.

In my idleness
sitting in the garden
going to seed
I consider
a single question:
shall I rise
and close the gate?

5.

Just after the 4th of July, an old friend and I traveled with our wives to hear a celebrated poet. The audience was large, filling a covered amphitheater. Two white-bearded cynics, we sat in the last row under the roof where the breeze was cool.

"He's a poet of sentiment," my friend said.

"Yes," I agreed. "He cleverly manages details and builds to a touching moment."

We visited the bookstore following the reading. No copy of his work remained for sale.

> In the shallows of the lily pond
> small fish—what can they know
> of winter or spring?
> —gold scales in the sun

6.

Some nights later I dreamed of a friend dead many years, a poet of brilliant intellect. He was not dead but had been living, protected by his wife, as a recluse hidden in the upstairs of his country house. Sometimes at night he walked in his garden. For a reason never explained he revealed himself to me. I asked if we might resume our exchange of letters. "Yes," he answered, "but not as before. I want to hear nothing of poetry. Write only of your garden."

At his death I had written

> Where did he go?
> Into the eye of quiet—
> tossed by the hurricane winds
> of the Spirit

7.

A tooth was causing me pain, so I took myself to the dentist. He determined I needed a crown. After much grinding, he paused and spoke. "You have what we call a short tooth. If I were you, I'd skip the cosmetic porcelain and simply have a metal crown."

"Fine with me," I said. "I'm trying to keep my mouth shut anyway."

Shall I interrogate my silence?

> Mindful of nothing
> but my brush
> I paint the ricks
> that will hold the wood
> that will hold the fire
> that will be light
> in the long cold

8.

In the 17th century Basho complained that he could write nothing to compare with the greatness of the writers he followed. Everything, he said, comes off as imitation. He wrote, "It is easy enough to say, for example, that such and such a day was rainy in the morning but fine in the afternoon, that there was a pine tree at such and such a place, or that the name of a river at a certain place was such and such, for these things are what everyone says in their diaries" (translated by Nobuyuki Yuasa).

I went hiking with a young poet who offered to accompany me on the last trail I had not walked along the river's gorge.

> I stood at Hog's Back Lookout—
> on the far peninsula point
> a stunted juniper

500 years old

At home

    In the wash
    of hummingbird wings
    I scrub from my ears
    ambition's buzz

9.

Considering the overgrown garden beds, I remember a teacher once told me if I would learn to write, I would need to learn what to keep out.

    Gathering basket
    in hand I swing
    the garden gate

Late Night: Thinking of William Carlos Williams, I Remember the Red Wheelbarrow and the Old Statue of St. Francis in the Shed

What does it matter, if I say
this or that—revise my poems,
wheel rocks from the river
to line the dry stream
through the garden,
pull weeds?

I come and go;
it's all the same—
one yielding.

When I mow the lawn,
I pause to urge small toads
from the mower's path.

When I'm awakened by the screech owl's
falling call, I lean out the window,
listen, answer, if necessary
with words.

Floating the River

When I first came to this valley smooth-faced
and eager, upstream rain raised the river
about my feet, isolating me yards
from shore on a grassy hammock
as I played a carp on broken tackle.
Undaunted, I made the river home,
floated its currents, learned its twists,
turns, and claimed the hidden solitude
of its overhanging banks. Now, with
my beard as white as the bright clouds
reflected in the water pooled at my feet,
the river has moved across the valley,
made the far shore an island shore,
and left this channel to beavers,
courting couples who embrace the grassy
edge mown park-like for their stroll,
and old men unfazed by time who sit
on beaver logs and watch the stillness
for Vs of change beneath the calm.

Wanting a Friend in Perilous Times

Old Friend, if you would journey here, you would
find the garden full but rain-pummeled,
the coneflowers and bee balm leaning
against each other, their colors fading.

The squash vines are dying, and soon I will dig
potatoes from their beds and store them
in the cool attic dark. Frost will sweeten the
brussels sprouts. Such flavors!

I should be at ease in my recluse
security, anticipating a holy death,
but dreams disturb my sleep; the death
that prowls is gaunt, untimely, and unjust.

It is the nought of all Creation,
the nought of sacrifice and exchange.
Bound by Love's tie to all that Love
has made, I wake to mourning.

Old Friend, if you would journey here, perhaps
we could laugh, proving the wreck of loss
is not loss, but evanescence, and fall
once more into that spontaneous obedience

to heaven's way on earth that opens
to the peace beyond all understanding.

for Jack Hazzard

Hand in Hand with the Daemon Meridianus

The garden frogs, anticipating winter,
have withdrawn from the rocks at the pond's edge.
Cats have invaded the yard
and driven the birds from the feeders.
Mornings and afternoons are silent.
The nation remains stubbornly at war
while maples flame in fleeting light.

A small-pond bureaucrat, I keep
a quiet office, move quietly
between work and leisure.
Acedia, that sin of worldly sorrow,
sits calling like a harmless dove
on my gravel path. Nights
I imagine peaceful recluse days—
days of spirit-touched mourning.

I go out into the half-moon dark
and walk the village streets:
lights flicker in unpeopled rooms,
an owl calls from Mouth of the Creek,
Flat Mountain is closed in clouds.

4 A.M. Meditation on the Baptism of Christ

Were this watch chosen, I would be still,
this wakefulness a quiet waiting
for the light rather than this agitation,
this restless tossing after sleep.

My dreams, too often dreamed
to appear strange, wake me. "Drill here.
Drill now," the nightmare politicians
chant as if the world were a tooth decayed:

native peoples float away
islands slip from underfoot
swimming bears tire and drown
in the rising tide of money money money.

The camel strains in the needle's eye.
Wanting ever more, the cheering crowd
will not yield even the riches
it cannot have. What have I to hold

against this dream? A cup of cold water.
A cup of blood. Crumbly bread
and the poverty of hope. Christ Jesus,
floating, swimming, going down.

Walking Beside the River the Afternoon of the Autumnal Equinox

Beavers raid the field, dragging dry cornstalks
down the bank to the quiet water
of the old oxbow, refreshed each rain
when runoff overflows the flood-straightened channel.

One day the news from the stock exchange
is good. The next day it is bad. Fortunes
rise and fall like the river. Floods come.
Cottonwoods fall in the stream.

Beavers trim the branches, tuck them
in their dams or store them up for winter.
Beside the still water, in the quiet mystery
of the beavers' imperturbable creating,

I tend my poverty, the inner pattern
of emptiness. Fortune comes and goes.
I am, at once, made and unmade in the awful
motion of the Maker's needless word.

The Night of the Hunter's Moon

From the disturbance of the great, lake city,
I fled south, up the river to Mouth of the Creek.
Driving the ridge, above the dividing gorge,
I drove between the Hunter's Moon rising
to the east and falling sun lighting vermillion
clouds to the west. Confucius said, *The virtuous*
love mountains; the wise love waters.
Dissolute in the perturbation of motion,
I descended to the valley at the deep cut,
where the dry canal leaves the riverside.

Darkness came to me. The familiar road,
dangerous with deer, settled my mind.
He who flees ought to know the place
to which he ought to flee. Bears roam here,
look in at screen doors. Coyotes bark
and squabble in the hills, pick off
wandering cats. Good for them!

Beyond Whisky Bridge, the takeout
before the falls for high-water drifters,
I slowed. *In flight is my beginning.*
I came to Mouth of the Creek,
talked quietly with my wife, sipped hibiscus tea.
The earlier form is lost in the change
of all things to a state of greater splendor.

Flat Mountain is never far.

On the Morning After the Killing Frost, I Discover Myself Almost Happy

Flat Mountain tends itself. Rain falls.
Leaves renew the soil. Seeds blow in
from everywhere, plant themselves, and grow.

Still, I putter about, shears in hand,
cutting down the dry delphinium,
the fading coneflowers, the frosted beans.

No one would call it working.
An armful here, an armful there,
and off to the compost pile.

No sweat. No hurry. Just a man,
troubled like every other
by news of crumbling institutions,

of uncertain futures floating
like smoke from the capitol.
Rain falls. Leaves renew the soil.

Flat Mountain tends itself. I mulch
the garden bed, with weathered hands,
join the ritual of seeds.

Awake in the Eternal Present

In my dream I dreamed I dreamed my poems.
When I woke, the bedside clock was flashing.
Lao Tzu's butterfly, a tiger swallowtail,
sat on the hand I reached out to touch
my sleeping wife. It walked from my finger
to bask in moonlight on her shoulder.

All this history!

Who can know beginnings or endings?
Real memories of what never happened
in this just-now-created world.

Walking the Circuit Around the Cornfield I Walk Every Day, I Glimpse the Nature of Creation and Submit to Joy

Beneath the intermittent buzz of cars
spinning down the two-lane,
of trucks rumbling home,
the constancy of water falling to the river
lives, a rocky song rising
over the silent corn.
In summer air the tassels are still.

Gnats swirl in the sharp light,
a constellation of dark amazements
turning about a moving center.

Though all creation groans,
the movement of the leaves
in the tallest cottonwoods
betrays the presence
of the wind:

the love that calls each moment forth
desires gnats and corn
and walkers blessed with ears and eyes.

In Flat Mountain Garden, the Word Becomes Flesh

One afternoon, the old man reading
beneath the larch is joined by a child.
He almost fails to notice,
she comes so silently,
barefoot through the grass.

She is carrying a book. She sits,
opens it without speaking.

Bluejays shriek, scold, pitch hard consonants
from the sun-blue berries
that are sugar on the empty tongue.

Hydrangeas lean in the wind
gesturing eloquently
to the buddleia;
their voices say other.
The jays', carry farther,
endure in the brightness.

The old man remains quiet.
The child remains mute. The larch thrives
in the mulch of their silence,
turns gold in time.

Invitation from Flat Mountain

One way to Mouth of the Creek
starts high and follows the water down.
Another way starts low and beats upstream.
Neither way is hard.
Getting lost is not an option.

No way, however, leads
to Flat Mountain. It keeps its summit
and its base well hidden,
moves where it chooses,
rewards no one for effort.

Meet me at Mouth of the Creek.
I keep a jug of water
in the fridge in case you find a thirst
along the way.

I have also wine and bread.
We can sit in the garden and say
the hours. Perhaps we will know
a shadow over us,
a motion beneath our feet,
or just the stillness holding fast.
Either will be grace. The mountain finds
all climbers. Getting lost
is not an option.

for Thom Satterlee

Flat Mountain Dream

Beyond Flat Mountain garden the high peaks.
Is it snow or cloud that tops their summits?
The eye cannot discern.

In the corner where the woods crowd close,
the old man has left open a gate.
He is bending over a bed pulling weeds.

Nearby, an older man, perhaps his father,
sits in the shade.
His hand holds a water bottle.

From the woods, a small bear emerges
and shambles toward the bending man.
Rising, the older man calls out,

but neither the old man nor the other man,
perhaps his father, moves.
The bear keeps coming.

The bending man cannot hear
the voice calling out. It is his dream,
and he knows the older man, who he sees

looks like his father, has been long dead
and can say nothing
the living can hear.

Is the old man living?
Is the bear real?
Of course the bear is real.

The man is living his dream.
He is happy looking over,
loving the silent man offering the bear water.

Waiting for Rain, I Remember
Three Old Poets Who Wandered the
Slopes of Flat Mountain in My Youth

In the afternoon wind the leaves turn
their pale undersides to the sky thickening
with clouds. It will rain by evening.

I walk slowly, easing my way
with the old stick that has let me
softly down many mountains.

Nothing pressing, free in the plenty
of time, I find my mind drifting
to thoughts of three old poets

who were bread and wine,
a sweet communion to my youth.
Each is gone, and I am old.

The first raised me from failure,
the second set me free,
the third gave me a snowy owl

and left a rifle in his will.
It never came.
The first discovered winter

a vast white emptiness and cursed
the hope that bound us from the start.
He threatened pills, but mercy

struck him by surprise.

The second disappeared without a word.
The third learned chaos,

raged against the loss of name
and place, and died uneasy
week by week then day by day

before the hour of forgiveness
covered him in sand.
I give thanks for my old stick,

its polished knob and thorny spikes.
it bends a bit under weight,
but it holds me up

as I bear these three through the wind-tossed
afternoon. I'll carry them awhile—
as far as heaven in my prayers.

Flat Mountain Folly

Who owns Flat Mountain?

Not you.
Not me.

We visit by invitation.
We stay by grace.

In spring we look around,
dig our fingers in the dirt,
talk to seeds
and little plants emerging in the light.

Oh, it is good. It is good.

Summer sun and summer rain
falls and falls.

What do we do?
What is good for us: open our hands,
taste and eat.

It is good. It is good.

One day, looking around, climbing the mountain,
we will come to the pavilion
festooned with flags and whirl-a-jigs
spinning in the wind.

It will be a great surprise,
for we will recognize we have many times stood
where it stands
and known nothing but the long view,

the distance we must go.

The owner will be weeping there.
Around him trees will be lifting up
their leaves in praise.

To our bewilderment he will shout:
"Come in! Come in!"

Suddenly we will discover ourselves
where we have always been,
one, by invitation and by grace, one
In the great crowd of his affection.
His weeping we will know
to be his joy at our inclusion,
and our hands lifted up
will be leaves
in the light of his presence.

Oh it is good. It is good.

A Casual Account of My Life at War at Mouth of the Creek

The nation falls into ruins;
rivers and mountains continue.
—Tu Fu

1.

The strength of one good eye
Unfit me for army life.

My draft board sent me home.
I came to this valley,

A reluctant scholar given more
To river travels and moonlight rambles

Than taking notes and giving
Back a master's words.

2.

I sought the word alone,
Sat nights beneath an oak

Solitary near the river,
Or waited on driftwood heaped

In the bend where the current
Turned away from town

And crossed the valley
Through the world of fox and owl.

3.

The word came sometimes to me,
And I cast nets of rhymes to hold

The grace elusive in its silence.
I need not say I failed. I failed.

Yet the movement of my lines
Ran like water through the land

I would become. It carved banks
And left seeds to grow in season.

4.

I went away. In a distant city,
Learning craft, I lived a hermit life.

Martin Luther King had a dream.
A bullet cut him down.

I saw my city burn. I mourned,
Stood confused by troops

Blockading the streets I knew
And walked just days before at ease.

5.

I returned clothed in the dark robe
Of a master to trail at the end

Of the scholars' solemn procession.
The river yet remained my home,

The oak a place of empty calm

In the chaos of daily dissolution.

In my poems the fox and owl
Conspired against the dark.

6.

In the capital LBJ, Rusk, and McNamara
Told each other lies and sent troops

To die by thousands. Monks burned
Themselves. Poets protested,

Destroying their poems with rage.
My brother fled the country,

And the word departed
From the discourse uttered in the news.

7.

That war divides us still. Some say
We lost it. Others say we simply lacked

The will to watch the necessary slaughter
To prevail. I say we lacked the nerve

To love our enemies as ourselves
And cross ourselves for peace.

I say, in Vietnam Christ died, and we
Have set in place his bondage stone.

8.

It rained. Not forty days and forty nights,

But long and hard. The river rose,

Topped its banks and spread
Across the valley. From the ridge

I looked down on water,
Houses filled to second storey windows.

The river cut through the bend, bore
Straight north through helpless corn.

9.
The Actor came to the capital, waged little wars
He could not lose, making once again

The bellicose attractive. He smiled
His way into the broken heart

That knew compassion and spun a tale
Of self-reliance. Poverty became

The sin too grievous to forgive.
The poor went underground.

10.
In the valley a posse of woodcutters
Stacked oak against the cold.

All winter they trucked rounds and splits
To widows and the old too cowed

To ask the state for help. My brother
In exile, I joined the opposition,

Traveled twice a year to the capital
To give words to the wordless.

11.

When the Iraqi thug with arms supplied
To keep Iran in check misread the signs

And stormed the oil fields of Kuwait,
Father Bush rose to defend

The interests of democracy. I joined
A delegation to the capital asking

For restraint. Our congressman was polite.
Days later he gave his voice to war.

12.

Back among the scholars, I found
The young men gone, called from their beds

At night. The war was short. Few
Whose names we know died.

Only enemies perished on the highway
Of death. We did not count their numbers.

Restrained, at last, we did not follow.
There were those who wished we had.

13.

My father fought a longer war
Where deaths were numbered

A million here, a million there.
They added up. My father's work

Was easy; he drove an ammo truck
And kept the guns engaged.

Father Bush knew that war
As well. Perhaps it held him back.

14.
"There are two kinds of drivers,"
my father told my brother.

"There are drivers who sleep
in fields far from their trucks,

and there are drivers who sleep
under them. I never liked the rain."

I remembered this one afternoon,
Walking the trail along the river.

15.
I remembered this one afternoon
In this time of endless storm.

In the beginning Dubya proclaimed
we must end the world of evil.

He gave us *shock and awe.*
We watched amazed as smart bombs,

Precise as the calculated lies he told,
Exploded in prime time.

16.

Each night the news displays the photos
Of the daily dead—*Give us this day*—

There aren't so many in this the longest
War of my life. Not millions anyway.

Only thousands, a few at a time.
Perhaps, if there were more—My father

Asked my brother, "How many bodies
Must you step over to know that war is wrong?"

17.

But there are more; the uncounted,
The unfigured lost in the pattern

Of frantic intention. The fox has a hole,
A den off the trail visible

To the good eye. Its kits look out
Trembling when I pass.

They cannot know my idleness
Is their protection.

18.

Forty years and more I have wandered
Listening for the word this valley speaks.

Forty years and more I have walked
In the procession of scholars,

Finally, in my fine robe, leading it.

Finally amused, trusting the world

To be what it will be. The Son of Man
Wants no where to lay his head.

19.
With my brother in exile, I have left
The procession. As it was

In the beginning, the wings of the owl
Feather the wind. The Spirit hovers

Over formlessness. The voice of Creation
Calls forth the listener.

Lightly, lightly. Go empty.
Hold nothing in the heart.

20.
The oak remains, still, solitary,
Dividing the corn from a newly landscaped

Playing field where youths compete
In games not far removed from war.

The river has left the channel empty,
Except for the flat of beaver water,

And courses down the valley
Half a mile away. Ever new, it remains.

Recluse Freedom

Master of ceremony, I led the procession
of scholars in my long robe.

What a joke!

My only virtue: not dying.
I'll soon fix that!

Today, however,

I'll haul firewood, climb Flat Mountain,
leap down the slope like a goat.

Other Books by John Leax

Poetry
Reaching into Silence
The Task of Adam
Country Labors
Tabloid News

Prose
In Season and Out
Standing Ground
Grace Is Where I Live
Out Walking

Fiction
Nightwatch

Chapbooks
A Proper Reticence
Finding the Word
Meditations on the Alphabet
Shoring the Ruins
The Fall's Discipline